Robert Louis Stevenson's

# A CHILD'S GARDEN OF VERSES

*ILLUSTRATED BY*
*HENRIETTE WILLEBEEK LE MAIR*

GALLERY CHILDREN'S BOOKS
LONDON

FOR OVER FIVE GENERATIONS, ROBERT LOUIS STEVENSON'S
*A CHILD'S GARDEN OF VERSES* HAS ENCHANTED AND CAPTURED
THE HEARTS OF READERS. TO A CHILD, THESE SIXTY-SEVEN
POEMS REFLECT THE FEELINGS, THOUGHTS AND DREAMS OF
CHILDHOOD; TO AN ADULT, THEY EVOKE LONG-FORGOTTEN
MEMORIES. STEVENSON COMPOSED THESE "PENNY WHISTLES,"
AS HE CALLED THEM, BETWEEN 1881 AND 1885. FIRST PUBLISHED
IN ENGLAND IN MARCH 1885, THEY WERE AN IMMEDIATE
SUCCESS AND HAVE NEVER BEEN OUT OF PRINT.

THE FIRST ILLUSTRATED EDITION OF THE WORK APPEARED IN
1895, A YEAR AFTER THE AUTHOR'S DEATH IN SAMOA AT THE AGE
OF FORTY-FOUR. SINCE THEN, MANY ARTISTS HAVE PRODUCED
ACCOMPANYING ILLUSTRATIONS TO THE TEXT; BUT FEW AS
SUCCESSFULLY AS THE INTERNATIONALLY RENOWNED DUTCH
ARTIST, HENRIETTE WILLEBEEK LE MAIR (1889-1966). LE MAIR'S
ABILITY TO CAPTURE THE SPIRIT OF CHILDHOOD THROUGH HER
DELICATE AND DECORATIVE DRAWINGS CREATED THE IDEAL
PARTNERSHIP WITH STEVENSON'S VERSES. ORIGINALLY
PUBLISHED IN 1926, THE PRESENT EDITION CONTAINS A NUMBER
OF ADDITIONAL DRAWINGS BY THE ARTIST TO RE-CREATE THIS
ENDURING CLASSIC FOR A NEW GENERATION.

# TO ALISON CUNNINGHAM

## FROM HER BOY

*FOR the long nights you lay awake*
*And watched for my unworthy sake:*
*For your most comfortable hand*
*That led me through the uneven land:*
*For all the story-books you read:*
*For all the pains you comforted:*
*For all you pitied, all you bore,*
*In sad and happy days of yore:—*
*My second Mother, my first Wife,*
*The angel of my infant life —*
*From the sick child, now well and old,*
*Take, nurse, the little book you hold!*

*And grant it, Heaven, that all who read*
*May find as dear a nurse at need,*
*And every child who lists my rhyme,*
*In the bright, fireside, nursery clime,*
*May hear it in as kind a voice*
*As made my childish days rejoice!*

R.L.S.

# CONTENTS

## A CHILD'S GARDEN

## THE CHILD ALONE

## GARDEN DAYS

## ENVOYS

# A CHILD'S GARDEN

IN winter I get up at night
And dress by yellow candle-light.
In summer, quite the other way,
I have to go to bed by day.

I have to go to bed and see
The birds still hopping on the tree,
Or hear the grown-up people's feet
Still going past me in the street.

And does it not seem hard to you,
When all the sky is clear and blue,
And I should like so much to play,
To have to go to bed by day?

IT is very nice to think
The world is full of meat and drink,
With little children saying grace
In every Christian kind of place.

## At the Seaside

WHEN I was down beside the sea
A wooden spade they gave to me
To dig the sandy shore.
My holes were empty like a cup,
In every hole the sea came up,
Till it could come no more.

H. Willebeek le Mair

ALL night long, and every night,
When my mamma puts out the light,
I see the people marching by,
As plain as day, before my eye.

Armies and emperors and kings,
All carrying different kinds of things,
And marching in so grand a way,
You never saw the like by day.

So fine a show was never seen
At the great circus on the green;
For every kind of beast and man
Is marching in that caravan.

At first they move a little slow,
But still the faster on they go,
And still beside them close I keep
Until we reach the town of Sleep.

A CHILD should always say what's true,
    And speak when he is spoken to,
And behave mannerly at table;
At least as far as he is able.

THE rain is raining all around,
 It falls on field and tree,
It rains on the umbrellas here,
 And on the ships at sea.

THREE of us afloat in the meadow by
     the swing,
  Three of us aboard in the basket on the lea.
Winds are in the air, they are blowing in the
     spring,
  And waves are on the meadow like the
     waves there are at sea.

Where shall we adventure, today that we're
     afloat,
  Wary of the weather and steering by a
     star?
Shall it be to Africa, a-steering of the boat,
  To Providence, or Babylon, or off to
     Malabar?

Hi! but here's a squadron a-rowing on the
     sea—
  Cattle on the meadow a-charging with a
     roar!
Quick, and we'll escape them, they're as
     mad as they can be,
  The wicket is the harbour and the garden
     is the shore.

UP into the cherry-tree
   Who should climb but little me?
I held the trunk with both my hands
And looked abroad on foreign lands.

I saw the next-door garden lie,
Adorned with flowers, before my eye,
And many pleasant places more
That I had never seen before.

I saw the dimpling river pass
And be the sky's blue looking-glass;
The dusty roads go up and down
With people tramping in to town.

If I could find a higher tree
Farther and farther I should see,
To where the grown-up river slips
Into the sea among the ships.

To where the roads on either hand
Lead onward into fairy land,
Where all the children dine at five,
And all the playthings come alive.

WHENEVER the moon and stars are set,
   Whenever the wind is high,
All night long in the dark and wet,
  A man goes riding by.
Late in the night when the fires are out,
Why does he gallop and gallop about?

Whenever the trees are crying aloud,
  And ships are tossed at sea,
By, on the highway, low and loud,
  By at the gallop goes he.
By at the gallop he goes, and then
By he comes back at the gallop again.

I SHOULD like to rise and go
Where the golden apples grow;—
Where below another sky
Parrot islands anchored lie,
And, watched by cockatoos and goats,
Lonely Crusoes building boats;—
Where in sunshine reaching out
Eastern cities, miles about,
Are with mosque and minaret
Among sandy gardens set,
And the rich goods from near and far
Hang for sale in the bazaar;—
Where the Great Wall round China goes,
And on one side the desert blows,
And with bell and voice and drum,
Cities on the other hum;—
Where are forests, hot as fire,
Wide as England, tall as a spire,
Full of apes and cocoa-nuts
And the negro hunters' huts;—
Where the knotty crocodile
Lies and blinks in the Nile,
And the red flamingo flies

Hunting fish before his eyes;—
Where in jungles, near and far,
Man-devouring tigers are,
Lying close and giving ear
Lest the hunt be drawing near,
Or a comer-by be seen
Swinging in a palanquin;—
Where among the desert sands
Some deserted city stands,
All its children, sweep and prince,
Grown to manhood ages since,
Not a foot in street or house,
Not a stir of child or mouse,
And when kindly falls the night,
In all the town no spark of light.
There I'll come when I'm a man
With a camel caravan;
Light a fire in the gloom
Of some dusty dining-room;
See the pictures on the walls,
Heroes, fights and festivals;
And in a corner find the toys
Of the old Egyptian boys.

OF speckled eggs the birdie sings
  And nests among the trees;
The sailor sings of ropes and things
  In ships upon the seas.

The children sing in far Japan,
  The children sing in Spain;
The organ with the organ man
  Is singing in the rain.

WHEN I am grown to man's estate
I shall be very proud and great,
And tell the other girls and boys
Not to meddle with my toys.

WE built a ship upon the stairs
All made of the back-bedroom chairs,
And filled it full of sofa pillows
To go a-sailing on the billows.

We took a saw and several nails,
And water in the nursery pails;
And Tom said, "Let us also take
An apple and a slice of cake;" —
Which was enough for Tom and me
To go a-sailing on, till tea.

We sailed along for days and days,
And had the very best of plays;
But Tom fell out and hurt his knee,
So there was no one left but me.

Dark brown is the river,
  Golden is the sand.
It flows along forever,
  With trees on either hand.

Green leaves a-floating,
  Castles of the foam,
Boats of mine a-boating—
  Where will all come home?

On goes the river
  And out past the mill,
Away down the valley,
  Away down the hill.

Away down the river,
  A hundred miles or more,
Other little children
  Shall bring my boats ashore.

WHENEVER Auntie moves around,
Her dresses make a curious sound;
They trail behind her up on the floor,
And trundle after through the door.

## The Land of Counterpane

WHEN I was sick and lay a-bed,
I had two pillows at my head,
And all my toys beside me lay
To keep me happy all the day.

And sometimes for an hour or so
I watched my leaden soldiers go,
With different uniforms and drills,
Among the bed-clothes, through the hills;

And sometimes sent my ships in fleets
All up and down among the sheets;
Or brought my trees and houses out
And planted cities all about.

I was the giant great and still
That sits upon the pillow-hill,
And sees before him dale and plain,
The pleasant land of counterpane.

H. Willebeek Le Mair

FROM breakfast on all through the day
At home among my friends I stay;
But every night I go abroad
Afar into the land of Nod.

All by myself I have to go,
With none to tell me what to do—
All alone beside the streams
And up the mountain-sides of dreams.

The strangest things are there for me,
Both things to eat and things to see,
And many frightening sights abroad
Till morning in the land of Nod.

Try as I like to find the way,
I never can get back by day,
Nor can remember plain and clear
The curious music that I hear.

I HAVE a little shadow that goes in and out
    with me,
And what can be the use of him is more
    than I can see.
He is very, very like me from the heels up
    to the head;
And I see him jump before me, when I jump
    into my bed.

The funniest thing about him is the way he
    likes to grow—
Not at all like proper children, which is
    always very slow;
For he sometimes shoots up taller like an
    india-rubber ball,
And he sometimes gets so little that there's
    none of him at all.

He hasn't got a notion of how children ought
    to play,
And can only make a fool of me in every sort
    of way.
He stays so close beside me, he's a coward
    you can see;
I'd think shame to stick to nursie as that
    shadow sticks to me!

One morning, very early, before the sun was
    up,
I rose and found the shining dew on every
    buttercup;
But my lazy little shadow, like an arrant
    sleepy-head,
Had stayed at home behind me and was fast
    asleep in bed.

EVERY night my prayers I say,
And get my dinner every day;
And every day that I've been good,
I get an orange after food.


The child that is not clean and neat,
With lots of toys and things to eat,
He is a naughty child, I'm sure—
Or else his dear papa is poor.

I WOKE before the morning, I was happy
  all the day,
I never said an ugly word, but smiled and
    stuck to play.

And now at last the sun is going down behind
  the wood,
And I am very happy, for I know that I've
  been good.

My bed is waiting cool and fresh, with linen
  smooth and fair,
And I must off to sleepsin-by, and not forget
  my prayer.

I know that, till to-morrow I shall see the
  sun arise,
No ugly dream shall fright my mind, no ugly
  sight my eyes,

But slumber hold me tightly till I waken in
  the dawn,
And hear the thrushes singing in the lilacs
  round the lawn.

THE lights from the parlour and kitchen
    shone out
  Through the blinds and the windows and
    bars;
And high overhead and all moving about,
  There were thousands of millions of stars.

There ne'er were such thousands of leaves
    on a tree,
  Nor of people in church or the Park,
As the crowds of the stars that looked down
    upon me,
  And that glittered and winked in the dark.

The Dog, and the Plough, and the Hunter,
    and all,
  And the Star of the Sailor, and Mars,
These shone in the sky, and the pail by the
    wall
  Would be half full of water and stars.

They saw me at last, and they chased me
    with cries,
  And they soon had me packed into bed;
But the glory kept shining and bright in
    my eyes,
  And the stars going round in my head.

BRING the comb and play upon it!
　　Marching, here we come!
Willie cocks his highland bonnet,
　　Johnnie beats the drum.

Mary Jane commands the party,
　　Peter leads the rear;
Feet in time, alert and hearty,
　　Each a Grenadier!

All in the most martial manner
　　Marching double-quick;
While the napkin like a banner
　　Waves upon the stick!

Here's enough of fame and pillage,
　　Great commander Jane!
Now that we've been round the village,
　　Let's go home again.

THE friendly cow all red and white,
  I love with all my heart:
She gives me cream with all her might,
  To eat with apple-tart.

She wanders lowing here and there,
  And yet she cannot stray,
All in the pleasant open air,
  The pleasant light of day;

And blown by all the winds that pass,
  And wet with all the showers,
She walks among the meadow grass
  And eats the meadow flowers.

THE world is so full of a number of
    things,
I'm sure we should all be as happy as kings.

I SAW you toss the kites on high,
  And blow the birds about the sky;
And all around I heard you pass,
Like ladies' skirts across the grass—
    O wind, a-blowing all day long,
    O wind, that sings so loud a song!


I saw the different things you did,
But always you yourself you hid.
I felt you push, I heard you call,
I could not see yourself at all—
    O wind, a-blowing all day long,
    O wind, that sings so loud a song!


O you that are so strong and cold,
O blower, are you young or old?
Are you a beast of field and tree,
Or just a stronger child than me?
    O wind, a-blowing all day long,
    O wind, that sings so loud a song!

OVER the borders, a sin without pardon,
  Breaking the branches and crawling
    below,
Out through the breach in the wall of the
  garden,
  Down by the banks of the river, we go.

Here is the mill with the humming of thunder,
  Here is the weir with the wonder of foam,
Here is the sluice with the race running
    under—
  Marvellous places, though handy to home!

Sounds of the village grow stiller and stiller,
  Stiller the note of the birds on the hill;
Dusty and dim are the eyes of the miller,
  Deaf are his ears with the moil of the mill.

Years may go by, and the wheel in the river
  Wheel as it wheels for us, children, to-day,
Wheel and keep roaring and foaming for ever,
  Long after all of the boys are away.

Home from the Indies and home from the
    ocean,
  Heroes and soldiers we all shall come home;
Still we shall find the old mill-wheel in
    motion,
  Turning and churning that river to foam.

You with the bean that I gave when we
    quarrelled,
  I with your marble of Saturday last,
Honoured and old and all gaily apparelled,
  Here we shall meet and remember the past.

CHILDREN, you are very little,
  And your bones are very brittle;
If you would grow great and stately,
You must try to walk sedately.

You must still be bright and quiet,
And content with simple diet;
And remain, through all bewild'ring,
Innocent and honest children.

Happy hearts and happy faces,
Happy play in grassy places—
That was how, in ancient ages,
Children grew to kings and sages.

But the unkind and the unruly,
And the sort who eat unduly,
They must never hope for glory—
Theirs is quite a different story!

Cruel children, crying babies,
All grow up as geese and gabies,
Hated, as their age increased,
By their nephews and their nieces.

LITTLE Indian, Sioux or Crow,
Little frosty Eskimo,
Little Turk or Japanee,
O! don't you wish that you were me?

You have seen the scarlet trees
And the lions over seas;
You have eaten ostrich eggs,
And turned the turtles off their legs.

Such a life is very fine,
But it's not so nice as mine;
You must often, as you trod,
Have wearied *not* to be abroad.

You have curious things to eat,
I am fed on proper meat;
You must dwell beyond the foam,
But I am safe and live at home.

Little Indian, Sioux or Crow,
Little frosty Eskimo,
Little Turk or Japanee,
O! don't you wish that you were me?

THE sun is not a-bed, when I
At night upon my pillow lie;
Still round the earth his way he takes,
And morning after morning makes.

While here at home, in shining day,
We round the sunny garden play,
Each little Indian sleepy-head
Is being kissed and put to bed.

And when at eve I rise from tea,
Day dawns beyond the Atlantic Sea,
And all the children in the West
Are getting up and being dressed.

MY tea is nearly ready and the sun has
        left the sky;
It's time to take the window to see Leerie
        going by;
For every night at tea-time and before you
        take your seat,
With lantern and with ladder he comes posting
        up the street.

Now Tom would be a driver and Maria go
        to sea,
And my papa's a banker and as rich as he
        can be;
But I, when I am stronger and can choose
        what I'm to do,
O Leerie, I'll go round at night and light the
        lamps with you!

For we are very lucky, with a lamp before
        the door,
And Leerie stops to light it as he lights so
        many more;
And O! before you hurry by with ladder and
        with light,
O Leerie, see a little child and nod to him
        to-night!

MY bed is like a little boat;
  Nurse helps me in when I embark;
She girds me in my sailor's coat
  And starts me in the dark.

At night, I go on board and say
  Good night to all my friends on shore;
I shut my eyes and sail away
  And see and hear no more.

And sometimes things to bed I take,
  As prudent sailors have to do;
Perhaps a slice of wedding-cake,
  Perhaps a toy or two.

All night across the dark we steer;
  But when the day returns at last,
Safe in my room, beside the pier,
  I find my vessel fast.

THE moon has a face like the clock in
the hall;
She shines on thieves on the garden wall,
On streets and fields and harbour quays,
And birdies asleep in the forks of the trees.

The squalling cat and the squeaking mouse,
The howling dog by the door of the house,
The bat that lies in bed at noon,
All love to be out by the light of the moon.

But all of the things that belong to the day
Cuddle to sleep to be out of her way;
And flowers and children close their eyes
Till up in the morning the sun shall arise.

# The Swing

HOW do you like to go up in a swing,
  Up in the air so blue?
Oh, I do think it the pleasantest thing
  Ever a child can do!


Up in the air and over the wall,
  Till I can see so wide,
Rivers and trees and cattle and all
  Over the countryside —


Till I look down on the garden green,
  Down on the roof so brown —
Up in the air I go flying again,
  Up in the air and down!

A BIRDIE with a yellow bill
Hopped upon the window-sill,
Cocked his shining eye and said:
"Ain't you 'shamed, you sleepy-head?"

SMOOTH it slides upon its travel,
 Here a wimple, there a gleam —
  O the clean gravel!
  O the smooth stream!

Sailing blossoms, silver fishes,
 Paven pools as clear as air —
  How a child wishes
  To live down there!

We can see our coloured faces
 Floating on the shaken pool
  Down in cool places
  Dim and very cool;

Till a wind or water wrinkle,
 Dipping marten, plumping trout,
  Spreads in a twinkle
  And blots all out.

See the rings pursue each other;
 All below grows black as night,
  Just as if mother
  Had blown out the light!

Patience, children, just a minute —
 See the spreading circles die;
  The stream and all in it
  Will clear by-and-by.

COME up here, O dusty feet!
　Here is fairy bread to eat.
Here in my retiring room,
　Children, you may dine

On the golden smell of broom
　And the shade of pine;
And when you have eaten well,
Fairy stories hear and tell.

## From a Railway Carriage

FASTER than fairies, faster than witches,
　Bridges and houses, hedges and ditches;
And charging along like troops in a battle,
All through the meadows the horses and
　cattle;
All of the sights of the hill and the plain
Fly as thick as driving rain;
And ever again, in the wink of an eye,
Painted stations whistle by.

Here is a child who clambers and scrambles,
All by himself and gathering brambles;
Here is a tramp who stands and gazes;
And there is the green for stringing the
　daisies!
Here is a cart run away in the road
Lumping along with man and load;
And here is a mill and there is a river;
Each a glimpse and gone for ever!

LATE lies the wintry sun a-bed,
A frosty, fiery sleepy-head;
Blinks but an hour or two; and then
A blood-red orange, sets again.

Before the stars have left the skies,
At morning in the dark I rise;
And shivering in my nakedness,
By the cold candle, bathe and dress.

When to go out, my nurse doth wrap
Me in my comforter and cap:
The cold wind burns my face, and blows
Its frosty pepper up my nose.

Close by the jolly fire I sit
To warm my frozen bones a bit;
Or with a reindeer sled, explore
The colder countries round the door.

Black are my steps on silver sod;
Thick blows my frosty breath abroad;
And tree and house, and hill and lake,
Are frosted like a wedding-cake.

THROUGH all the pleasant meadow-side
  The grass grew shoulder-high,
Till the shining scythes went far and wide
  And cut it down to dry.

These green and sweetly smelling crops
  They led in waggons home;
And they piled them here in mountain tops
  For mountaineers to roam.

Here is Mount Clear, Mount Rusty-Nail,
  Mount Eagle and Mount High;—
The mice that in these mountains dwell,
  No happier are than I!

O what a joy to chamber there,
  O what a place for play,
With the sweet, the dim, the dusty air,
  The happy hills of hay.

THE coach is at the door at last;
The eager children mounting fast
And kissing hands, in chorus sing:
Good-bye, good-bye, to everything!

To house and garden, field and lawn,
The meadow-gates we swang upon,
To pump and stable, tree and swing,
Good-bye, good-bye, to everything!

And fare you well for evermore,
O ladder at the hayloft door,
O hayloft where the cobwebs cling,
Good-bye, good-bye, to everything!

Crack goes the whip, and off we go;
The trees and houses smaller grow;
Last, round the woody turn we swing;
Good-bye, good-bye, to everything!

*I—Good Night*

WHEN the bright lamp is carried in,
The sunless hours again begin;
O'er all without, in field and lane,
The haunted night returns again.

Now we behold the embers flee
About the firelit hearth; and see
Our faces painted as we pass,
Like pictures, on the window-glass.

Must we to bed indeed? Well then,
Let us arise and go like men,
And face with an undaunted tread
The long black passage up to bed.

Farewell, O brother, sister, sire!
O pleasant party round the fire!
The songs you sing, the tales you tell,
Till far to-morrow, fare ye well!

## II—Shadow March

All round the house is the jet-black night;
  It stares through the window-pane;
It crawls in the corners, hiding from the light,
  And it moves with the moving flame.

Now my little heart goes a-beating like a drum,
  With the breath of the Bogie in my hair;
And all round the candle the crooked shadows come
  And go marching along up the stair.

The shadow of the balusters, the shadow of the lamp,
  The shadow of the child that goes to bed—
All the wicked shadows coming, tramp, tramp, tramp,
  With the black night overhead.

## III—In Port

Last, to the chamber where I lie
My fearful footsteps patter nigh,
And come from out the cold and gloom
Into my warm and cheerful room.

There, safe arrived, we turn about
To keep the coming shadows out,
And close the happy door at last
On all the perils that we past.

Then, when mamma goes by to bed,
She shall come in with tip-toe tread,
And see me lying warm and fast
And in the Land of Nod at last.

# THE CHILD ALONE

WHEN children are playing alone on
    the green,
In comes the playmate that never was seen.
When children are happy and lonely and good,
The Friend of the Children comes out of the
    wood.

Nobody heard him and nobody saw,
His is a picture you never could draw,
But he's sure to be present, abroad or at home,
When children are happy and playing alone.

He lies in the laurels, he runs on the grass,
He sings when you tinkle the musical glass;
Whene'er you are happy and cannot tell why,
The Friend of the Children is sure to be by!

He loves to be little, he hates to be big,
'T is he that inhabits the caves that you dig;
'T is he when you play with your soldiers of
    tin
That sides with the Frenchmen and never
    can win.

'T is he, when at night you go off to your bed,
Bids you go to your sleep and not trouble your head;
For wherever they're lying, in cupboard or shelf,
'T is he will take care of your playthings himself!

O IT'S I that am the captain of a tidy
   little ship,
Of a ship that goes a-sailing on the pond;
And my ship it keeps a-turning all around
   and all about;
But when I'm a little older, I shall find the
   secret out
    How to send my vessel sailing on beyond.

For I mean to grow as little as the dolly at
   the helm,
  And the dolly I intend to come alive;
And with him beside to help me, it's a-sailing
   I shall go,
It's a-sailing on the water, when the jolly
   breezes blow
    And the vessel goes a divie-divie dive.

O it's then you'll see me sailing through the
   rushes and the reeds,
  And you'll hear the water singing at the
    prow;
For beside the dolly sailor, I'm to voyage and
   explore,
To land upon the island where no dolly was
   before,
    And to fire the penny cannon in the bow.

DOWN by a shining water well
    I found a very little dell,
  No higher than my head.
The heather and the gorse about
In summer bloom were coming out,
  Some yellow and some red.

I called the little pool a sea;
The little hills were big to me;
  For I am very small.
I made a boat, I made a town,
I searched the caverns up and down,
  And named them one and all.

And all about was mine, I said,
The little sparrows overhead,
  The little minnows too.
This was the world and I was king;
For me the bees came by to sing,
  For me the swallows flew.

I played there were no deeper seas,
Nor any wider plains than these,
  Nor other kings than me.
At last I heard my mother call
Out from the house at evenfall,
  To call me home to tea.

And I must rise and leave my dell,
And leave my dimpled water well,
  And leave my heather blooms.
Alas! and as my home I neared,
How very big my nurse appeared,
  How great and cool the rooms.

SUMMER fading, winter comes —
Frosty mornings, tingling thumbs,
Window robins, winter rooks,
And the picture story-books.

Water now is turned to stone
Nurse and I can walk upon;
Still we find the flowing brooks
In the picture story-books.

All the pretty things put by,
Wait upon the children's eye,
Sheep and shepherds, trees and crooks,
In the picture story-books.

We may see how all things are,
Seas and cities, near and far,
And the flying fairies' looks,
In the picture story-books.

How am I to sing your praise,
Happy chimney-corner days,
Sitting safe in nursery nooks,
Reading picture story-books?

THESE nuts, that I keep in the back of
    the nest
Where all my lead soldiers are lying at rest,
Were gathered in autumn by nursie and me
In a wood with a well by the side of the
    sea.

This whistle we made (and how clearly it
    sounds!)
By the side of a field at the end of the
    grounds.
Of a branch of a plane, with a knife of my
    own,
It was nursie who made it, and nursie alone.

The stone, with the white and the yellow and
    grey,
We discovered I cannot tell *how* far away;
And I carried it back although weary and
    cold,
For though father denies it, I'm sure it is
    gold.

But of all of my treasures the last is the king,
For there's very few children possess such a
    thing;
And that is a chisel, both handle and blade,
Which a man who was really a carpenter
    made.

WHAT are you able to build with your blocks?
Castles and palaces, temples and docks.
Rain may keep raining, and others go roam,
But I can be happy and building at home.

Let the sofa be mountains, the carpet be sea,
There I'll establish a city for me;
A kirk and a mill and a palace beside,
And a harbour as well where my vessels may ride.

Great is the palace with pillar and wall,
A sort of a tower on the top of it all,
And steps coming down in an orderly way
To where my toy vessels lie safe in the bay.

This one is sailing, and that one is moored:
Hark to the song of the sailors on board!
And see on the steps of my palace, the kings
Coming and going with presents and things!

Now I have done with it, down let it go!
All in a moment the town is laid low.
Block upon block lying scattered and free,
What is there left of my town by the sea?

Yet as I saw it, I see it again,
The kirk and the palace, the ships and the men;
And as long as I live, and where'er I may be,
I'll always remember my town by the sea.

AT evening when the lamp is lit,
Around the fire my parents sit;
They sit at home and talk and sing,
And do not play at anything.

Now, with my little gun, I crawl
All in the dark along the wall,
And follow round the forest track
Away behind the sofa back.

There, in the night, where none can spy,
All in my hunter's camp I lie,
And play at books that I have read
Till it is time to go to bed.

These are the hills, these are the woods,
These are my starry solitudes;
And there the river by whose brink
The roaring lions come to drink.

I see the others far away
As if in firelit camp they lay,
And I, like to an Indian scout,
Around their party prowled about.

So, when my nurse comes in for me,
Home I return across the sea,
And go to bed with backward looks
At my dear land of Story-books.

THE lamps now glitter down the street;
Faintly sound the falling feet;
And the blue even slowly falls
About the garden trees and walls.

Now in the falling of the gloom
The red fire paints the empty room;
And warmly on the roof it looks,
And flickers on the backs of books.

Armies march by tower and spire
Of cities blazing, in the fire; —
Till as I gaze with staring eyes,
The armies fade, the lustre dies.

Then once again the glow returns;
Again the phantom city burns;
And down the red-hot valley, lo!
The phantom armies marching go!

Blinking embers, tell me true
Where are those armies marching to,
And what the burning city is
That crumbles in your furnaces!

WHEN at home alone I sit
And am very tired of it,
I have just to shut my eyes
To go sailing through the skies —
To go sailing far away
To the pleasant Land of Play;
To the fairy land afar
Where the Little People are;
Where the clover-tops are trees,
And the rain-pools are the seas,
And the leaves like little ships
Sail about on tiny trips;
And above the daisy tree
  Through the grasses,
High o'erhead the Bumble Bee
  Hums and passes.

In that forest to and fro
I can wander, I can go;
See the spider and the fly,
And the ants go marching by
Carrying parcels with their feet
Down the green and grassy street.
I can in the sorrel sit
Where the ladybird alit.
I can climb the jointed grass;
    And on high
See the greater swallows pass
    In the sky,
And the round sun rolling by
Heeding no such things as I.

Through that forest I can pass
Till, as in a looking glass,
Humming fly and daisy tree
And my tiny self I see,
Painted very clear and neat
On the rain-pool at my feet.
Should a leaflet come to land
Drifting near to where I stand,
Straight I'll board that tiny boat
Round the rain-pool sea to float.

Little thoughtful creatures sit
On the grassy coasts of it;
Little things with lovely eyes
See me sailing with surprise.
Some are clad in armour green —
(These have sure to battle been!) —
Some are pied with ev'ry hue,
Black and crimson, gold and blue;
Some have wings and swift are gone; —
But they all look kindly on.

When my eyes I once again
Open, and see all things plain;
High bare walls, great bare floor;
Great big knobs on drawer and door;
Great big people perched on chairs,
Stitching tucks and mending tears,
Each a hill that I could climb,
And talking nonsense all the time —
　　O dear me,
　　That I could be
A sailor on the rain-pool sea,
A climber in the clover tree,
And just come back, a sleepy-head,
Late at night to go to bed.

# GARDEN DAYS

WHEN the golden day is done
  Through the closing portal,
Child and garden, flower and sun,
  Vanish all things mortal.

As the blinding shadows fall,
  As the rays diminish,
Under evening's cloak, they all
  Roll away and vanish.

Garden darkened, daisy shut,
  Child in bed, they slumber —
Glow-worm in the highway rut,
  Mice among the lumber.

In the darkness houses shine,
  Parents move with candles;
Till on all, the night divine
  Turns the bedroom handles.

Till at last the day begins
  In the east a-breaking,
In the hedges and the whins
  Sleeping birds a-waking.

In the darkness shapes of things,
  Houses, trees, and hedges,
Clearer grow; and sparrows' wings
  Beat on window ledges.

These shall wake the yawning maid;
  She the door shall open —
finding dew on garden glade
  And the morning broken.

There my garden grows again
  Green and rosy painted,
As at eve behind the pane
  From my eyes it fainted.

Just as it was shut away,
  Toy-like, in the even,
Here I see it glow with day
  Under glowing heaven.

Every path and every plot,
  Every bush of roses,
Every blue forget-me-not
  Where the dew reposes,

"Up!" they cry, "the day is come
  On the smiling valleys;
We have beat the morning drum;
  Playmate, join your allies!"

Birds all the sunny day
  Flutter and quarrel
Here in the arbour-like
  Tent of the laurel.

Here in the fork
  The brown nest is seated;
Four little blue eggs
  The mother keeps heated.

While we stand watching her,
  Staring like gabies,
Safe in each egg are the
  Bird's little babies.

Soon the frail eggs they shall
  Chip, and upspringing
Make all the April woods
  Merry with singing.

Younger than we are,
  O children, and frailer,
Soon in blue air they'll be,
  Singer and sailor.

We, so much older,
  Taller and stronger,
We shall look down on the
  Birdies no longer.

They shall go flying
  With musical speeches
High overhead in the
  Tops of the beeches.

In spite of our wisdom
  And sensible talking,
We on our feet must go
  Plodding and walking.

A LL the names I know from nurse:
  Gardener's garters, Shepherd's purse,
Bachelor's buttons, Lady's smock,
And the Lady Hollyhock.

Fairy places, fairy things,
Fairy woods where the wild bee wings,
Tiny trees for tiny dames—
These must all be fairy names!

Tiny woods below whose boughs
Shady fairies weave a house;
Tiny tree-tops, rose or thyme,
Where the braver fairies climb!

Fair are grown-up people's trees,
But the fairest woods are these;
Where if I were not so tall,
I should live for good and all.

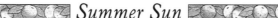

Great is the sun, and wide he goes
Through empty heaven without repose;
And in the blue and glowing days
More thick than rain he showers his rays.

Though closer still the blinds we pull
To keep the shady parlour cool,
Yet he will find a chink or two
To slip his golden fingers through.

The dusty attic, spider-clad,
He, through the keyhole, maketh glad;
And through the broken edge of tiles,
Into the laddered hayloft smiles.

Meantime his golden face around
He bares to all the garden ground,
And sheds a warm and glittering look
Among the ivy's inmost nook.

Above the hills, along the blue,
Round the bright air with footing true,
To please the child, to paint the rose,
The gardener of the World, he goes.

WHEN the grass was closely mown,
   Walking on the lawn alone,
In the turf a hole I found
And hid a soldier underground.

Spring and daisies came apace;
Grasses hide my hiding-place;
Grasses run like a green sea
O'er the lawn up to my knee.

Under grass alone he lies,
Looking up with leaden eyes,
Scarlet coat and pointed gun,
To the stars and to the sun.

When the grass is ripe like grain,
When the scythe is stoned again,
When the lawn is shaven clear,
Then my hole shall reappear.

I shall find him, never fear,
I shall find my grenadier;
But, for all that's gone and come,
I shall find my soldier dumb.

He has lived, a little thing,
In the grassy woods of spring;
Done, if he could tell me true,
Just as I should like to do.

He has seen the starry hours
And the springings of the flowers;
And the fairy things that pass
In the forests of the grass.

In the silence he has heard
Talking bee and ladybird,
And the butterfly has flown
O'er him as he lay alone.

Not a word will he disclose,
Not a word of all he knows.
I must lay him on the shelf,
And make up the tale myself:

IN the other gardens
  And all up the vale,
From the autumn bonfires
  See the smoke trail!


Pleasant summer over,
  And all the summer flowers,
The red fire blazes,
  The grey smoke towers.


Sing a song of seasons!
  Something bright in all!
Flowers in the summer,
  Fires in the fall!

THE gardener does not love to talk,
He makes me keep the gravel walk;
And when he puts his tools away,
He locks the door and takes the key.

Away behind the currant row
Where no one else but cook may go,
Far in the plots, I see him dig,
Old and serious, brown and big.

He digs the flowers, green, red, and blue,
Nor wishes to be spoken to.
He digs the flowers and cuts the hay,
And never seems to want to play.

Silly gardener! summer goes,
And winter comes with pinching toes,
When in the garden bare and brown
You must lay your barrow down.

Well now, and while the summer stays,
To profit by these garden days,
O how much wiser you would be
To play at Indian wars with me!

DEAR Uncle Jim, this garden ground,
   That now you smoke your pipe around,
Has seen immortal actions done
And valiant battles lost and won.

Here we had best on tip-toe tread,
While I for safety march ahead,
For this is that enchanted ground
Where all who loiter slumber sound.

Here is the sea, here is the sand,
Here is simple Shepherd's Land,
Here are the fairy hollyhocks,
And there are Ali Baba's rocks.

But yonder, see! apart and high,
Frozen Siberia lies; where I,
With Robert Bruce and William Tell,
Was bound by an enchanter's spell.

There, then, a while in chains we lay,
In wintry dungeons, far from day;
But ris'n at length, with might and main,
Our iron fetters burst in twain.

Then all the horns were blown in town;
And, to the ramparts clanging down,
All the giants leaped to horse
And charged behind us through the gorse.

On we rode, the others and I,
Over the mountains blue, and by
The Silver River, the sounding sea,
And the robber woods of Tartary.

A thousand miles we galloped fast,
And down the witches' lane we passed,
And rode amain, with brandished sword,
Up to the middle, through the ford.

Last we drew rein—a weary three—
Upon the lawn, in time for tea,
And from our steeds alighted down
Before the gates of Babylon.

# ENVOYS

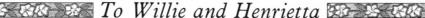

IF two may read aright
These rhymes of old delight
And house and garden play,
You two, my cousins, and you only, may.

You in a garden green
With me were king and queen,
Were hunter, soldier, tar,
And all the thousand things that children are.

Now in the elders' seat
We rest with quiet feet,
And from the window-bay
We watch the children, our successors, play.

"Time was," the golden head
Irrevocably said;
But time which none can bind,
While flowing fast away, leaves love behind.

YOU too, my mother, read my rhymes
For love of unforgotten times,
And you may chance to hear once more
The little feet along the floor.

## To Auntie

CHIEF *of our aunts*—not only I,
*But all your dozen of nurslings cry—*
*What did the other children do?*
*And what were childhood, wanting you?*

THE red room with the giant bed
Where none but elders laid their head;
The little room where you and I
Did for a while together lie,
And, simple suitor, I your hand
In decent marriage did demand;
The great day nursery, best of all,
With pictures pasted on the wall
And leaves upon the blind —
A pleasant room wherein to wake
And hear the leafy garden shake
And rustle in the wind —
And pleasant there to lie in bed
And see the pictures overhead —
The wars about Sebastopol,
The grinning guns along the wall,
The daring escalade,
The plunging ships, the bleating sheep,
The happy children, ankle-deep
And laughing as they wade:
All these are vanished clean away,
And the old manse is changed to-day;
It wears an altered face
And shields a stranger race.

The river, on from mill to mill,
Flows past our childhood's garden still;
But ah! we children never more
Shall watch it from the water-door!
Below the yew — it still is there —
Our phantom voices haunt the air
As we were still at play,
And I can hear them call and say:
*"How far is it to Babylon?"*

Ah, far enough, my dear,
Far, far enough from here —
Yet you have farther gone!
*"Can I get there by candlelight?"*
So goes the old refrain.
I do not know — perchance you might —
But only, children, hear it right,
Ah, never to return again!
The eternal dawn, beyond a doubt,
Shall break on hill and plain,
And put all stars and candles out,
Ere we be young again.

To you in distant India, these
I send across the seas,
Nor count it far across.
For which of us forgets
The Indian cabinets,
The bones of antelope, the wings of albatross,
The pied and painted birds and beans,
The junks and bangles, beads and screens,
The gods and sacred bells,
And the loud-humming, twisted shells?
The level of the parlour floor
Was honest, homely, Scottish shore;
But when we climbed upon a chair,
Behold the gorgeous East was there!
Be this a fable; and behold
Me in the parlour as of old,
And Minnie just above me set
In the quaint Indian cabinet!
Smiling and kind, you grace a shelf
Too high for me to reach myself.
Reach down a hand, my dear, and take
These rhymes for old acquaintance' sake.

## 1

SOME day soon this rhyming volume, if
  you learn with proper speed,
Little Louis Sanchez, will be given you to
  read.
Then shall you discover, that your name was
  printed down
By the English printers, long before, in
  London town.

In that great and busy city where the East
  and West are met,
All the little letters did the English printer
  set;
While you thought of nothing, and were still
  too young to play,
Foreign people thought of you in places far
  away.

Ay, and while you slept, a baby, over all the
  English lands
Other little children took the volume in their
  hands;

Other children questioned, in their homes
  across the seas:
Who was little Louis, won't you tell us,
  mother, please?

## 2

Now that you have spelt your lesson, lay it
  down and go and play,
Seeking shells and seaweed on the sands of
  Monterey,
Watching all the mighty whalebones, lying
  buried by the breeze,
Tiny sandy-pipers, and the huge Pacific seas.

And remember in your playing, as the sea-
  fog rolls to you,
Long ere you could read it, how I told you
  what to do;
And that while you thought of no one, nearly
  half the world away
Some one thought of Louis on the beach of
  Monterey!

AS from the house your mother sees
   You playing round the garden trees,
So you may see, if you will look
Through the windows of this book,
Another child, far, far away,
And in another garden, play.
But do not think you can at all,
By knocking on the window, call
That child to hear you. He intent
Is all on his play-business bent.
He does not hear; he will not look,
Nor yet be lured out of this book.
For, long ago, the truth to say,
He has grown up and gone away,
And it is but a child of air
That lingers in the garden there.